School Violence

Deadly Lessons

Francha Roffé Menhard

Enslow Publishers, Inc.

40 Industrial Road PO Box 38
Box 398 Aldershot
Berkeley Heights, NJ 07922 Hants GU12 6BP
USA UK

http://www.enslow.com

For those who died at Columbine High School
and for those who survived.

Acknowledgments

Thanks to all those who helped me with this book: Mollie and Richard Arthur; Wes Ashley; Sallie Baier; Yolanda Bezio; Greg and Jan Glazner, and their daughter, Pam, who survived the massacre at Columbine; Bill Head; Erica Alikchihoo in *Newspapers in Education*; John Moore and Lori Punko in the sports department at *The Denver Post*; Ken, Steven, and Jennifer Rappe; Vicki Salazar; and Dr. Nicole Sperekas.

Library of Congress Cataloging-in-Publication Data

Menhard, Francha Roffé.
    School violence: deadly lessons/ Francha Roffé Menhard.
        p. cm. – (Teen issues)
    Includes bibliographical references and index.
    Summary: Recounts some of the heinous acts of violence in America's schools, explains why people resort to this type of behavior, and discusses ways to avoid such tragedies.
    ISBN 0-7660-1358-8
    1. School violence—United States—Juvenile literature. [1. School violence.
2. Violence] I. Title. II. Series.

LB3013.3 .M46 2000
371.7'82'0973 21 –dc21   99-043566
                                              CIP

Printed in the United States of America

10 9 8 7 6 5 4 3 2 1

To Our Readers:
All Internet addresses in this book were active and appropriate when we went to press. Any comments or suggestions can be sent by e-mail to Comments@enslow.com or to the address on the back cover.

Illustration Credits: Courtesy of Melanie Stephens, pp. 13, 16, 23, 28, 33, 35, 36, 43; Francha Roffé Menhard, p. 4, 8, 19.

Cover Illustration: Portrait by Ed French; Background © Corel Corporation.

Contents

Two students at Columbine High School read the memorial poster for the students who were killed in the 1999 shooting by two of their fellow students. The students, Dylan Klebold and Eric Harris, fatally shot themselves after they murdered thirteen people.

1

Columbine

The graffiti in the bathroom read: "Columbine will explode in one day. . . . All jocks must die."[1]

Tuesday, April 20, 1999, 11:21 A.M.

Columbine High School, Jefferson County, Colorado

Hundreds of students ate lunch or stood in line for free cookies in the cafeteria. Others prepared for a concert in the choir room or studied in classrooms or in the library. Just outside the cafeteria door, Eric Harris and Dylan Klebold began their deadly rampage. They shot Danny Rohrbough first, then laughed, hooted, and taunted classmates as they set off bombs, injured more than twenty people, and killed twelve students and one teacher.

Terrified teens crawled along the floor toward exits and

then ran for their lives. Others hid in closets or barricaded themselves inside classrooms. Some students inside the school watched the unbelievable drama unfolding on television or called for help on cell phones. Many wrote notes to their parents and friends, telling them how much they loved them.[2] In one science classroom, students used their shirts to try to staunch the flow of blood from business teacher Dave Sanders, who died that day.[3] Outside, parents waited in gridlock traffic or at a nearby school for life-or-death news.

The Killers

The two shooters had a lot in common with the boys who shot up schools from Pearl, Mississippi, to Bethel, Alaska. They were fascinated with weapons and violence. A veteran of Doom, which bills itself as a "gun-toting, testosterone-pumping, cold-blooded murdering" computer game, Eric Harris modified several games to represent Columbine High School. Such games are equivalent to those the military uses to increase the rate at which soldiers shoot to kill in battle, says Lieutenant Colonel David Grossman, a psychologist who recently retired from the United States Army. Eric and Dylan practiced until killing became a reflex.[4] In the aftermath of the tragedy, authorities said they confiscated a copy of the school floor plan from Harris's house that noted good places to hide and spots with poor lighting.

The Spiral of Rejection

By the end of the day, the world had begun to hear disturbing reports of the Trenchcoat Mafia, a group of outcast Columbine students who had created an identity by combining countercultural ideas and fads.[5] Later in the week, stories of the hell Eric and Dylan had lived through during high school began to make news. For years "jocks"—student athletes—persecuted them, said Joe Stair, a friend of theirs,[6] calling them nasty names and throwing bottles and rocks at them from moving cars.[7] Finally, Eric did not care if he lived or died,[8] and Dylan was willing to follow his friend and fellow outcast into the valley of death at age seventeen. A friend said, "These guys were just pushed too far."[9]

No one believes that harassment by jocks excuses what the boys did at Columbine. But some of the parents and students there said that the school's tolerance of criminal acts, physical abuse, and sexual and racial bullying by some jocks intensified the killers' feelings of powerlessness and strengthened their fantasies of revenge.[10]

It Could Not Happen Here

As with previous shootings, there was the familiar refrain: "We never thought it could happen here." Columbine was such a good school in such a nice suburb—just like Jonesboro, Arkansas; just like Moose Lake, Washington. Nobody thought it could happen there, either. Nobody anywhere thinks it could happen here.

Jennifer does not think it could happen at her urban high school, where fights and pulled fire alarms are daily rituals, where lunchroom and parking lot brawls are common, and a stabbing almost killed one freshman. "Anybody who came in and started shooting," Jennifer said, "there'd have been at least thirty kids pulling loaded guns out of their waistbands and shooting back."[11] It could not happen in her small rural school, either, said Barbara (not her real name). "Everybody's friends with everybody," she said, "and nobody seems to have the mean gene."[12]

Students who survived the fatal shootings at Columbine High School try to console each other at a memorial service for their slain friends.

It Could Happen Here

Michael Sheehan knows that it could happen here. He has experienced both sides of the deadly equation. In middle school, Michael's classmates made fun of his shoes and his lack of athletic ability. It hurt a lot. As the student body president for the 1999–2000 school year at Columbine High School, Michael used his office to "bridge the Berlin Walls of separation" that divide students. During the summer of 1999, he asked his friends to reach out and invite classmates they barely knew to parties, to include them in their groups, and to say hello in the halls in an effort to break down some of the cliques that can turn students into alienated, angry outcasts.[13]

Safe Schools

In spite of random mass murders and other highly publicized violence, schools are still among the safest places for teens. But any violence in school is too much violence. One random shooting, assault, rape, hate crime, or robbery adds to the fear that many teens face when going to school. Steps must be taken to end the violence. The responses to the questions below will affect teens throughout their school career.

- What is the source of the violence?
- How common is violence?
- What kind of person resorts to violence at school?
- What is happening at other schools?
- What are communities doing about violence in schools? What do they plan to do?
- What can students do to create safer schools?

2

The Problem

School violence does not start at school. Students bring what they learn at home and in their communities to school with them. And life is not easy in many homes and communities. Abusive parents raise children who perpetuate the cycle of violence. Parents who spend every minute earning a living do not have the time to teach their children how to deal with frustration and conflict. Some parents have time but do not spend it with their children. The example some parents set teaches children to distrust authority, to hate people who are different, or to use violence to solve problems.

Jason (not his real name) stomped on six cars during a homecoming brawl in the west parking lot of a big city high school. The school's principal learned of Jason's vandalism when a yearbook photographer gave him copies of photos she had taken of Jason. The principal called in Jason's dad and showed him the evidence. Jason's dad was furious. But not at Jason. He wanted the name of the photographer. He wanted to sue her and the school for invading his son's privacy.[1]

The Media and Violence

From the time they are old enough to watch cartoons, American kids overdose on violence. Television does not make children commit acts of violence, but it does numb them to the horror of violence and convinces them that violent behavior is normal.[2] According to a recent study, 47 percent of violent acts on television do not harm the victim. Eighty-six percent of violent acts have no negative repercussions: No one dies, no one goes to jail, no one's life is ruined. And 73 percent of the time, the perpetrator of television violence goes unpunished.[3]

Our society *teaches* children to kill each other. The media make violence look glamorous. "From your very first cartoon through *Lethal Weapon 3*, society has told teens that 'violence is the hero's way to solve the problem: Hit back. Be the Rambo,'" said Deborah Prothrow-Stith, a national authority on violence.[4]

In 1991, shootings at Brooklyn's Thomas Jefferson High School left one student dead and a teacher wounded. That same week, the television show *Saturday Night Live* turned the tragedy into a comedy skit. "There were no tears, funerals, or images of kids crying in teachers' arms" in the skit, says Linda Lantieri, cofounder of New York City's Resolving Conflict Creatively Program.[5] On television, violence is entertainment. So when real violence happens, it does not seem all that terrible. Fights at school seem like good entertainment—a break from boredom and routine.

Weapons: The Adolescent Arms Race

Weapons—especially guns—make the world a dangerous place for teens. In 1995, the last year for which statistics are available, firearms accounted for 29 percent of the deaths of teens between the ages of fifteen and nineteen.[6] More than 8 percent of students have carried a gun to school in one school month and more than 7 percent have been threatened or injured with a gun at school in one school year, according to the Centers for Disease Control.[7] That translates to more than ten people under age twenty who die in gunfire every day. No wonder teens across the country are arming themselves. And teens often need to look no farther than the bedroom down the hall for a gun. Homes across the country—43 percent of homes with children—have guns.[8]

Most students who bring guns to school do not plan on using them. But the presence of a gun increases the odds of deadly violence when trouble starts. Highly publicized school shootings in Arkansas, Mississippi, Oregon, and Colorado have made students across the country very aware of the danger they face from guns.

In 1998 millions of students across the country participated in the annual Day of National Concern about Gun Violence. Some students marched in silence. Others wore black armbands to represent young people killed with guns every day in America. By November 1998 over a million more had signed a pledge circulated nationwide not to take guns to school.[9] But that did not stop Eric Harris and Dylan Klebold from setting off bombs at Columbine High School and killing twelve of their classmates five months later.

The Substance Abuse Connection

Students are no strangers to the use of alcohol and drugs. Almost 80 percent have tried alcohol at least once in their lives and more than half have had a drink in any given month, according to the Centers for Disease Control. One third drink heavily, and almost one third have been offered, sold, or given an illegal drug on school property in the past year.[10] More than one third of middle school students and more than one half of high school students have tried some kind of illicit drug.[11] Drug and alcohol abuse—even a one-time experience—can contribute to school violence.

At Carmel High School in Indiana, students who are suspended from school have to submit to a drug test before they can return. That school's experience shows that 40 percent of students suspended for fighting and 42 percent of those suspended for smoking test positive for using illegal drugs.[12]

Weapons and drug paraphernalia confiscated from students at a large urban high school.

Drugs impair judgment. They make people less inhibited. They slow down reaction time. Students who would normally find a peaceful way to deal with the conflicts that are part of every school day cannot think clearly when they are under the influence of drugs. Students on drugs may become bolder and head into a fight they would normally avoid. They may be too slow to avoid a punch—or a knife. Even students who do not take drugs are at increased risk when other students use, buy, or sell drugs. A drug deal goes bad. One student fails to pay. The student who sold him the drugs retaliates in the hallway or locker room. Or a seller from a rival gang moves into a school, and innocent bystanders get caught in the crossfire.

How Much School Violence Is There?

School violence directly affects more than half of American schools, and the shadow of violence affects all of them. Almost 60 percent of public schools reported fighting, theft, larceny, and vandalism.[13] One third have had personal property deliberately damaged or stolen at school in the past year.[14] Twenty percent of middle and high schools reported serious crimes—robberies (seven thousand one hundred), fights with weapons (eleven thousand), sexual assault, and rape (four thousand one hundred).

In general, large schools, poor schools, and schools in urban areas report the most violence. High schools and middle schools have more violence than elementary schools.[15] One in seven middle and high school students have been the victims of violence—assault, theft, robbery, or bullying. About one in eight students in middle and high school has been the victim of such violence.

Every hour more than two thousand students are physically attacked, nine hundred teachers are threatened, and forty teachers are physically attacked on school grounds, according to the U.S. Department of Justice.[16] One in nine students stayed away from school in 1997 for fear of being beaten or shot. In high crime areas, that number rose to one in three. One in eight students carried a weapon to school for protection. In high crime areas, the number was almost one in two.[17] According to the National School Safety Center, from July 1992 to the end of the 1998 school year, 211 school violence–related deaths occurred in thirty-eight states and Washington, D.C.[18]

The Human Cost of School Violence

Violence starts a vicious circle. Violence creates fear and anxiety. Fear and anxiety increase hopelessness. Hopelessness increases inaction. Inaction increases hostility. Hostility increases violence. And around and around.

Students

Students do not have to be physically attacked to suffer from violence at school. Students who are afraid often find it hard to study and learn. They miss school more often[19] and are more likely to carry weapons for protection. In high crime areas, four students in ten carry a weapon. One in eight male students and one in twenty-six female students carries a weapon.[20] Students who actually live and attend school in dangerous areas exhibit the "same signs of post-traumatic stress syndrome that we observe in children who grow up in war-torn areas," said Carol Beck, former principal of Thomas Jefferson High School in Brooklyn, New York.[21]

Teachers are afraid of violence, too, and with good reason. Each year between 1992 and 1996, an average of eighteen thousand teachers were victims of serious crime at school.[22] Teachers in violent schools miss more days of

Security guards are increasingly common in American schools.

school than teachers who feel safe at school. Some are too intimidated to stand up to troublemakers. They close their eyes to conflicts between students, because they know that if they try to intervene in a violent situation, they may become victims themselves. Other teachers give up. They quit or find jobs in safer schools that can afford to pay them more.

The Financial Cost of School Violence

School violence is expensive. In 1996, Texas spent more than $80 million on school security. Most of the money went for police officers and security guards. Some eighty school districts in Texas have their own police force. Other money went for technology—metal detectors and cameras. The statewide total spent on security came to twenty-one dollars per student.

That may not seem like much, but it is money that schools could have spent on something else. Houston, for example, spent more money on security (thirty-six dollars per student) than on sports and all nonclassroom activities put together (thirty-five dollars). And the cost of security is rising.

Texans believe the money is well spent. They want safe schools and they are willing to pay for them.[23] But for every metal detector that schools buy, there are computers, baseball bats, uniforms, or trumpets that they cannot buy. For every police officer that a school hires, there is a teacher or a coach whom it cannot hire. One of the sad trade-offs is that spending dollars on security turns schools into prisons while it dries up money for the activities that make schools fun.

3

Trouble at School

*V*iolence from outsiders is also scary because it is random, and school staff and students have little control over it. Some outsiders come to school to steal. Others come looking for a gang rival or a romantic competitor. And divorced parents who do not have custody of their children have been known to kidnap them from their classrooms.

For someone planning to attack or kill a student, school is the logical place to go looking, school police officer Theresa Garagin told *Spank!*, an online teen magazine: "School is the one place kids know you're going to be from 8:30 [A.M.] to 3:30 [P.M.] every day."[1] That is where a student, Hugo, was killed. As he sat in front of a computer at his alternative school in Illinois, a masked man walked into his classroom, pulled out a gun, and killed him.[2] Police labeled it a gang shooting. Weeks later, the police still had not caught the gunman.

Gang Members and Wanna-Bes

Gangs have been on the American scene for a long time. Philadelphia had children's gangs in 1791. Big eastern cities had them in the mid-1800s. In the early 1900s, children who poured into the cities looking for work banded together for protection and companionship. During Prohibition, gangs of adult mobsters who sold illegal alcohol recruited members from youth street gangs. Crime boss Al Capone got his start this way.[3]

Today, the United States Office of Juvenile Justice estimates that there are some thirty-one thousand street gangs in the United States, with a membership of almost nine

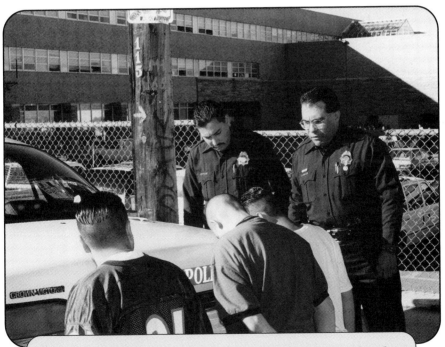

Students sometimes join gangs to gain a sense of identity, but that identity often comes at the price of peace.

hundred thousand young people. Ninety percent of gang members are male.[4] Gangs affect communities of all sizes in all fifty states and Washington, D.C. Cities are still most likely to report gang activity, followed by suburban areas. In recent years, however, more and more gangs have shown up in smaller cities and in rural areas.

Gangs can cause a lot of trouble for schools. Middle and high school students tend to form cliques—exclusive groups that usually exclude all but a few classmates. The cliques compete for status and popularity. Students on the outside of these cliques are easy targets for gang members, who offer them a group of their own to which they can belong.

And when gangs compete for status at school, trouble usually begins. Members of rival gangs can start something by "set tripping," in which gang members use their hands to display signs rather than colors to identify their particular gang.[5] Set tripping leads to fights, which can end up involving innocent bystanders.

Gangs that deal in drugs bring another set of problems into a school. Disagreements over sales and payment often lead to violence. And the more students use drugs, the greater the likelihood of violence in a school. Drugs are the business of choice for gangs. The federal Office of Justice Programs estimates that gangs are involved in 43 percent of all illegal drug sales in the United States,[6] and classmates are logical customers.

The Protection Racket

With all of the fear and violence that gangs cause, it is hard for many adults to understand why teens join them. But the reasons have not changed in the past two centuries. Teens still feel they need protection, and they still need a place to belong. Also, as schools become more violent, students feel more need for protection. If adults at school cannot or will not keep them safe, they will find someone who will.

A seventeen-year-old named Cory said, "Kids fighting and threatening other kids—that stuff is not going to change. Every year it gets worse. Me and a bunch of other guys started a gang to protect ourselves. . . . As long as there are people who want to pick on other people, there are people that will fight back."[7]

Being "Bad"

Some teens join gangs because gangs are macho, according to Sergeant Jerry Flowers, president of the Oklahoma Gang Investigators Association. "It's like a status symbol, like you are saying, 'I'm bad, so don't mess with me.'"[8]

Miguel (not his real name) was like that. The driving force in his life was to make a name for himself. Nobody noticed him much until he joined his school newspaper staff and acquired a reputation as an investigative reporter. Miguel liked seeing his name in print, and he liked the feeling of asking hard questions and getting them answered. The next year, he could not fit journalism into his schedule. Without his newspaper, Miguel thought he was a nobody. Miguel looked around for something else to pump up his name. He found a start-up gang that wanted to make its mark on the west side of a large city.

One December day, Miguel and several other gang members opened a tear-gas canister outside the lunchroom. As a column of smoke surrounded them, students wheezed, coughed, and gagged. They left their lunches and ran for the exits. Teachers in a third-floor lounge broke windows and escaped to the roof. The principal canceled afternoon classes, and the school stayed closed the next day.[9]

The school had already seen its share of stink and

smoke bombs that fall, but Miguel wanted to put his gang on the map. He wanted to show everybody that his gang could shut down the school whenever it wanted. The students involved were convicted of felonies.

Trouble Inside Schools

Most serious trouble on campus is caused by 3 to 6 percent of students, according to some sociologists, but that small group can come up with many ways of spreading misery. And it only takes a few minutes to terrorize an entire school.[10]

The Bully Factor

Brian Head had a poster of Martin Luther King's "I Have a Dream" speech on the wall of his bedroom. He loved his parents and told them so every day. He wrote poetry and plays for his drama class. He played video games on his computer. He went camping, fishing, and hunting.

Brian liked wearing camping and hunting gear to school. He wore thick glasses. He was big at fifteen, already five feet eleven inches and overweight, and classmates picked on him for that. Sometimes, his father said, it got so bad that when Brian got off the bus in the afternoon, he sat on the lawn and cried. His parents talked to teachers and to the principal, but the abuse continued. Teachers said Brian should solve his own problems, and his friends were too intimidated to defend him. By his sophomore year, Brian stopped complaining. His parents thought everything was all right. But a small group of students continued to hound Brian, harassing him verbally, putting signs on his back, hitting him, and pulling his hair.

One day Brian had had enough. He pulled a 9 mm Beretta semiautomatic from his backpack and waved it around his economics classroom. He said, "I'm tired of it," put the gun to his head, and pulled the trigger.[11]

Misery at the Hands of Bullies

Bullying probably causes more pain for more young people than all of the other forms of school violence combined. Most bullying is verbal rather than physical. Still, its effect on victims is devastating. Nearly 7 percent of eighth graders stay home at least once a month because of bullies.[12]

After a thirteen-year-old student died as a result of bullying, the principal at Booth Middle School in Cherokee County, Georgia, surveyed nine hundred students. The results: One third of the girls and half of the boys considered bullying a problem. One quarter of the girls and one third of

Angela's childhood friend committed suicide. "She hated school," said Angela. "She was so sad the last time I saw her."

the boys had witnessed verbal bullying. One in twelve girls and one in ten boys had witnessed physical bullying.[13]

The Bullies

Bullies take advantage of less powerful people. Some bullies, such as those who are athletes, draw their power from their physical size and strength, but bullies also depend on street smarts or social skills.

Bullies look for reasons to pick on others. They will interpret a potential victim's actions as hostile whether or not they are. That gives them an excuse to pick on someone. Once they lock onto a victim, bullies are merciless. Low on compassion and unable to connect with how other people are feeling, they find it easy to convince themselves that their bad behavior is the victim's fault.[14] That is why they can be so convincing about their innocence if a victim tells an adult.

But bullies are not particularly brave. They only take on situations where they are sure to win. They also back themselves up with "henchmen"[15]—a group that supports and will sometimes do their dirty work for them. Bullies also depend on a conspiracy of silence among classmates who watch and do nothing to stop them.

Bully Bait

There are two kinds of victims. Passive victims are often small and sensitive. They usually have few friends, lack social skills, and may cry easily. Others may feel sorry for them, but they do not want to stand up for them against a bully. That makes it easy for bullies to pick on them.[16]

On the other hand, most students do not have much sympathy for provocative victims. Classmates usually do not stand up for them because they do not like them. Provocative victims know what buttons to push to annoy classmates and irritate adults. Clumsy, immature, and restless, they may have trouble learning. Provocative victims are often quick-tempered. When a bully picks on them, they fight back, but they lose to the bully in the end.[17]

Stopping Bullies in Their Tracks

The accepted advice on stopping bullies is to tell an adult. But there are problems with this advice. Victims often do not want adults to know. Being bullied is humiliating, and victims may think the bullying is probably their own fault. Besides, they do not really believe adults can do anything. And adult interference might make things worse.

As long as bullies get what they want through intimidation and violence, they will keep it up. But allowing bullies to get away with their behavior can be dangerous. Students who have watched and said nothing run the risk of becoming the bully's next victim. And when they do, will anybody in the group stand up for them? Probably not. Another danger is that students are the ones who are most likely to get caught in the crossfire when a victim has had enough and comes to school to take revenge with a gun in his or her hand.

Bystanders: Breaking the Silence

It is important for teens to break the cycle of bullying. Students can go to an adult and demand that the bully be stopped. Bullies are usually good at hiding their actions, and without evidence, adults cannot act. If teens want to stop this common form of violence, they must find the courage to make sure that adults have the evidence they need. To be more effective, entire groups of students can stand up to bullies. When bullies do not have henchmen and silent conspirators, they usually find another way to entertain themselves.

Victims: Fighting Back

Some victims of bullies have found relief by staying away from the bully and trying to avoid being found alone. Sometimes the personal, direct approach can stop bullies. Some recommendations:

- Walk tall and act confident
- Try not to react
- Make a joke of the bully's taunts
- Say, "Cut it out," and walk away
- Hang out with a group
- Ask friends to stand up to the bully
- Tell parents and teachers
- Get away and get safe if the bully threatens to turn violent[18]

The behavior that adds up to bullying is common in schools, but anywhere else, it would be considered criminal. Every state, county, and town has laws against harassment, stalking, or assault and battery. Teens, with the help of their parents, can take advantage of existing laws to force bullies to take responsibility for their actions.

Bill Head, whose son Brian committed suicide after being bullied for years, suggests that victims of bullies and their parents follow these steps to deal with bullying:

1. Keep a record of what happened in each incident of bullying.

2. Get a copy of the state criminal code as well as county and local ordinances.

3. Find out what the laws say about assault, battery, stalking, harassment, physical violence—the kind of bullying that is happening. Lawyers can provide the same information for a fee.

4. Document the following for each incident:

   - Date and location

   - Exactly what happened

   - Names and ages of everyone involved in incidents, including witnesses

   - Pictures that show cuts, bruises, or bodily harm

   - A statement of how the incident violated the law

   - The law that applies and its reference number.

This documentation will come in handy if it is necessary to file criminal charges.[19]

Fights

Fights without weapons are the most common form of school violence. Almost 40 percent of students get into one or more physical fights on school property each year, according to the Centers for Disease Control.[20]

Everybody has seen it: She looked at her. He bumped into him in the hall. Next thing, a fight starts. Students gather, jostling for a spot in the front row. Students in the back stand on tiptoe to watch each punch. Somebody starts yelling, "Fight, fight, fight."

Most violent encounters start with something trivial—mean looks, teasing, put-downs, unwelcome touching, or rough play. Once the challenge is issued, the "sucker phenomenon"[21] kicks in. The sucker phenomenon demands that teens retaliate or join a fight out of loyalty.[22] At this point it is hard to back down. Students have to defend their honor in front of an audience. Half the time students fight in spots where they know no adult will stop them.

Fights can destroy lives. Students can face criminal charges or end up injured or dead. Students who want to reduce school violence have to make it uncool to fight by refusing to watch fights and by calling in an adult before someone gets hurt.

Hate Crime on Campus

Hate crime is violence motivated by hatred based on race, ethnicity, religion, national origin, or sexual orientation. It can be carving a swastika into the desk of a Jewish student,

Fights that begin with mean looks and rude comments can end up with a trip to jail.

shouting slurs at Asians, or beating up a gay person. The FBI reports that there were more than eight thousand reported victims of hate crime in the United States in 1997, though not only in schools.[23]

American schools have increasingly diverse student bodies, and bigoted students can spark violence. And it only takes two angry students to start a brawl like the one that broke out at California's Inglewood High School. Festering anger over Black History Month and *Cinco de Mayo* celebrations led to bottle throwing and a brawl at a nearby park. Police used pepper spray to break it up and arrested five students.

Teens at Huntington Beach High School in California decided to take a stand against hate. For several years students have held a Walk for Peace on Main Street. Before their 1997 walk, teens attended a retreat where they discussed ways to get members of all of the different groups on campus involved.

They worked together with city officials, the police

Facts About Hate Crime

- Most hate crimes are based on race
- Most hate crime is committed by young people
- One third of hate crimes involve physical assault
- Hate crimes are often extremely brutal and cause serious injuries

Source: Richard Verdugo, *Hate Motivated Crime and Violence*, National Education Association, 1998, <http://www.nea.org/issues/safescho/hatecrim.html> (June 9, 1999).

department, and parents to plan their Walk for Peace. Groups of students who had never even talked before worked together.[24] Huntington Beach teens learned something very important: If teens are going to survive in the twenty-first century, now is the time to learn to get along with the student sitting at the next desk.

Sexual Violence

In the old days, when Vince's name was in the paper, it was for carrying the offense for his New York City school football team. That all changed one April day when his friend DeShawn lured Tanya (not her real name), a freshman, to Room 324 at lunchtime. He said he wanted to tell her something about a friend—in private. She knew

---

How to Avoid a Fight

- Control your temper
- Think about what is triggering the fight
- Understand that sometimes people use fighting to make themselves feel better, so treat the other student as a decent human being
- Try to appeal to the other student's sense of decency
- If the other student does not respond, walk away
- Use gentle humor if possible

Source: Thomas J. Collins, "The Fight That Never Ends Fueled by a Cycle of Revenge, Teen Violence Is at an Alarming Level in the Twin Cities," *St. Paul Pioneer Press*, December 7, 1997.

DeShawn, so she did not think too much about going with him. Big mistake. Vince and two friends were waiting in the unused classroom.

While teammate Charles held Tanya down, Vince, DeShawn, and another friend, Valjean, took turns raping her. Right away the rumors started to fly. The boys bragged about the attack. The next day, some of Tanya's friends told a counselor about the rape. The day after, Tanya told the same counselor and an assistant principal.

Nothing happened. No one at school got Tanya counseling or medical treatment. No one called her parents or the police. No one changed the lock on the door of Room 324. It was not until a month later, after Tanya reported the rape again—to yet another assistant principal—that someone called the police, who arrested Vince and his friends.

The gang rape of Tanya did not have to happen. It was no secret that students could get into Room 324, a classroom with asbestos problems that had supposedly been locked up for four years. According to court documents, members of the football team had a tradition of using the key and the room. The morning of the rape, a teacher and a custodian had found a hall pass and used condoms there. The teacher reported it immediately—in writing—to three assistant principals and a dean, but no one bothered to check.[25]

Students Harassing Students

Most sexual violence in schools is more subtle than rape. It is sexual harassment that shakes its victims' confidence and makes school a scary place to be. Sexual harassment goes all the way from sexual looks to lewd comments and jokes, gestures, and unwelcome touching. Sexual harassment is very common. Most girls first experience sexual abuse in school. More than 80 percent of students in grades eight through eleven have been sexually harassed at least once, according to a survey by the American Association of University Women.

Girls suffer more from sexual harassment at school than boys do, and it makes them lose confidence and feel afraid to go to school, according to the survey. Most students were reluctant to talk to adults about sexual harassment. Sixty-three percent confided in a friend, but only 23 percent told an adult in their family, and fewer than 10 percent told a teacher about sexual harassment.[26]

While some school officials are reluctant to follow through on sexual harassment complaints, most know that effective action is their best defense. Schools can be held liable only if they do not respond quickly and effectively to stop the harassment, the Supreme Court ruled in May 1999.[27]

Gay and lesbian students also suffer harassment, threats, and violence at school, and that harassment starts early. Bullies often use homosexuality to justify their hate crimes. "The captain of the football team met me in the hallway," a teen remembers. "He said, 'You can't go by me, faggot.' I dropped the art project I was carrying and he beat the crap out of me."

Even teachers and staff can be insensitive and cruel to students they know are gay and lesbian. "I actually had a teacher, as I walked by his desk, whisper under his breath, 'God forgive her,'" a lesbian teen said, "as if I were sinning just being alive."[28]

Protection From Sexual Harassment

Ignoring sexual harassment will not make it go away. Victims must find the courage to stand up for themselves. Telling a harasser to cut it out—loudly, in front of other

Is it flirting or harassment? If welcome, it is flirting and it is fun. But if the other person indicates a lack of interest or annoyance or seems upset at the attention, it is harassment.

people—can sometimes be embarrassing enough to make a harasser stop.

If the harassment continues, teens should enlist the moral support of friends and parents. They should also keep a diary of what happens and when, and they should complain in writing to their principal, superintendent, and each member of their school board. (Principals should be able to provide addresses.) Students and their parents should keep copies of all correspondence.

Sexual harassment is against the law. If school officials will not act, or if the harassment takes place both at and away from school, teens can file a complaint with police, file a civil lawsuit, or ask a judge for a restraining order.

Lawsuits and restraining orders are a last resort. Students should first talk to teachers, counselors, and principals about problems at school. A teen's most effective weapon in fighting sexual harassment is telling an adult.

Bombs and Bomb Threats

The increase in bomb threats and unscheduled fire drills in recent years has frazzled school administrators across the country. Students have suffered interrupted classes, canceled activities, and hours of waiting outside in all kinds of weather. The Jonesboro, Arkansas, teens who pulled a fire alarm and then opened fire as their classmates filed out of the school added fear to the annoyance of mass evacuations of students from school buildings.

Deadly Violence

Students across the country watched with shock and horror as students with guns murdered and wounded dozens of their classmates throughout the United States between 1997 and 1999. On May 21, 1998, Kip Kinkel killed two students in the lunchroom at Thurston High School in Springfield, Oregon, just hours after murdering his parents. He wounded twenty-three more students before classmates tackled him and held him for police.

Nobody saw it coming, although there had been warning signs. Kip was isolated and angry, and his classmates knew it. His middle school yearbook called him the student "most likely to start World War III." Fascinated with violence and weapons, Kip bragged about torturing animals and showed off a pipe bomb he kept in his locker.[29]

Kip told classmates and teachers that he was ready to hurt people. In his English class, he read from his journal about his plans to "kill everybody."[30] Kip's friend Destry

A pipe bomb found in an empty classroom forced students to evacuate the school.

said that Kip had talked about putting a bomb under the bleachers at a pep rally and blocking the door so no one could get out. His friend thought he was just joking. He told another friend, Mike, "When I snap, I want the firepower to kill people." But Mike missed the warning sign, too. Even when Kip talked about spraying the cafeteria with bullets, Destry did not take him seriously.[31]

Who Will Explode?

It is easy to talk about all the warning signs people missed after a student goes on a rampage, but predicting who is going to explode is like predicting volcanoes. People know the volcano is there. They may even hear rumbling or see a plume of ash from time to time. But no one can predict

A student sits at a desk covered with items left in memory of a good friend who is now dead, a victim of school violence.

Multiple Victim School Shootings in the United States

Year	School	Location	Dead
1992	Langham Creek High School	Houston, Texas	2
1993	East Carter High School	Grayson, Kentucky	2
	Weatherless Elementary School	Washington, D.C.	2
1995–96	Olathe North High School	Olathe, Kansas	2
	Blackville-Hilda High School	Blackville, South Carolina	2
	Richland High School	Lynnville, Tennessee	2
	Frontier Junior High School	Moses Lake, Washington	3
	Beaumont High School	St. Louis, Missouri	2*
1996–97	Smedley Elementary School	Philadelphia, Pennsylvania	2
	Bethel Regional High School	Bethel, Alaska	2
1997–98	Pearl High School	Pearl, Mississippi	2
	John Glenn High School	Norwalk, California	2
	Heath High School	West Paducah, Kentucky	3
	Hoboken High School	Hoboken, New Jersey	2
	Westside Middle School	Jonesboro, Arkansas	5
	Philadelphia Elementary School	Pomona, California	2
	Thurston High School	Springfield, Oregon	2
	Stranahan High School	Ft. Lauderdale, Florida	2
1998–99	Columbine High School	Jefferson County, Colorado	15†

*A pregnant teen

†The number of deaths includes the two killers.

Source: Associated Press, 1999.

precisely when the volcano will explode—or if it will. But there are signs teens can look for.

Psychologists have developed a profile of the kind of teen who is likely to commit the kind of violence that Kip Kinkel did. He is a male. As a child, he practiced his cruelty on animals. He seems to have a grudge against the school or against his classmates. Add access to handguns and a recent humiliation, and look out![32]

As students at Thurston High School and other high schools across the country have learned, teens need to speak up about the warning signs they see.

4

Making School a Better Place

More than half of the students at Kentucky's Hopkinsville High School told their youth services center that they did not feel comfortable talking to teachers or administrators about drugs at school. Almost half said it was not their responsibility to report drugs at school.[1] But if students want safer schools, they must take responsibility and exercise power they may not realize they have.

Behaving Responsibly

The easiest—and maybe the hardest—thing that teens can do is to behave responsibly at school by knowing and following school rules, treating students and teachers with respect and kindness, and settling disagreements nonviolently. Teens can do a lot to create a nonviolent atmosphere by avoiding the kind of behaviors that trigger the most common form of school violence, fights. These behaviors include mean looks, name calling, trash talking, sarcastic remarks, put-downs, and spreading rumors.

The kind of put-downs that teens hear daily on television sitcoms and radio talk shows do nothing to create a positive peer culture. But they are second nature to teens who feel they have to put other people down to prop themselves up. The put-down culture that dominates most schools does nothing to create a safe and pleasant environment. A kind word or two can sometimes defuse situations that might explode into violence.

Jen was sitting in the library, trying hard to solve a trigonometry problem. A girl she barely knew demanded to know what *she* was looking at. Jen wanted to snarl back, but she stopped herself. Instead she told the girl she was looking at the girl's shirt, told her she thought it was so cute, and asked her where she had gotten it.

Fast thinking? Not really. Mean looks caused a lot of fights at Jen's school, and fighting was not something she wanted to do. So, she practiced ahead of time. She knew pretty much what she would say if anyone ever came at her with "What are *you* looking at?"[2]

Listening to each other, respecting other students' personal space, swearing off rumors, accusations, sarcasm, and aggressive gestures, and solving problems in private—these are some other steps teens can take to create a positive peer culture. In some schools, students have declared certain areas "no put-down zones." Friends monitor each other and give signals if they hear negative talk.

Reaching Out in Friendship

In the weeks after the shootings at Columbine High School, thousands of teens logged on to Internet chat rooms and message boards to express empathy with the killers and to talk about the misery and hopelessness of being an outcast. A common theme among the messages was: "That could have been me," and "I could be the next to snap."

A self-defined outcast who graduated in the early 1990s said, "A kid I knew from study hall offered to sell me a gun. I envisioned myself walking through the halls . . . killing everyone who ever beat me up, made fun of me, or ignored me. I knew then I had a way to make them all pay. One thing stopped me. I couldn't cough up the $50."[3]

The sheer number of similar postings should make students think about reaching out, or at least being kind, to teens who seem different. The loner in the second row could be dreaming of payback and might have access to weapons to back up his or her fantasy.

Staying Out of Harm's Way

Nobody knows better than teens that no one has control over everything that happens at school. But the decisions that students make can increase or reduce their chances of becoming victims.

Safety-savvy students are aware of their environment. They stay with a group and avoid the places where school violence is most likely to happen—stairways, halls, and locker rooms. They do not come to school under the influence of drugs or alcohol. They mind their own business. They do not start fights. They do not bring weapons to school. They choose their friends wisely, avoiding gangs and gang members and students who are just at school to cause trouble.

Steve went to the worst school in his city. Gang graffiti was everywhere—inside and outside of the school—and nobody bothered to clean it up. There was at least one fight each day. Sometimes fights turned into chair-throwing riots in the lunchroom or ethnic brawls in the parking lot. Still, Steve managed to stay out of trouble and get a good education.

Steve said,

> I had friends that were not into fighting. I hung out with that group. I've seen my share of fights, but I was not ever in the first six rows of kids watching. And I never joined the yelling. You know, "Fight! Fight! Fight!" A couple of times things went over the top. I got out of there and told a teacher before somebody got killed.[4]

Students can also stay out of harm's way by taking action against violent students who victimize them.

Turning to Adults for Help

There seems to be an unwritten taboo against tattling to adults. Some teens keep quiet out of loyalty to friends. Others fear retaliation. Some just do not want to get involved. But in this day of deadly violence in schools, students need to break the code of silence.

Part of maturity is knowing the difference between tattling and telling. "Children tattle to get their own way," says Alan McEvoy, a professor who works with the Safe Schools Coalition. Responsible teens "tell an adult to keep themselves or someone else from getting hurt."[5]

Students who do not tell may live to regret their silence when a friend goes ballistic and ruins his or her life with a spray of bullets. Students who keep silent may die when violence they feared actually happens.

Teachers and school staff are as eager as teens are to be safe at school. They know that intervention is easier and more effective when problems are small, and they appreciate whatever information students are willing to give them. They take threats seriously and have the power to do something about them.

Wise teachers and administrators understand that teens know much more about what is going on at school than adults ever will. They depend on information from students to make them aware of security gaps and to help them protect students.

Students have a right to feel safe at school. If there is something that makes them feel unsafe, they must speak up. Teens can get their student government involved, write a letter to their school and community newspapers, speak to the school board, or pass a petition. Where their safety is

When a problem arises that could lead to violence, students should talk with a teacher or an adult they trust.

concerned, students must demand action and refuse to be ignored.

Solving Problems When Adults Will Not Help

Some principals deal with school violence by pretending it does not exist. If nobody talks about it, they think, it will not happen. Sometimes, principals are so concerned about their school's reputation that they do not take steps to deal with violence for fear of bad publicity. This is frustrating for teens and their teachers, who feel helpless to do

Tips From Students Help to Avert Possible Mass Murders

Burlington, Wisconsin, November 15, 1998—Police arrested five students after classmates told them the students had guns and a list of students and teachers they planned to kill.

Concord, New Hampshire, January 7, 1999—A sophomore at Bishop Brady High School was charged with two felonies after students told school officials that he had a loaded handgun and two hundred rounds of ammunition in his locker. Police also found a hit list with names of students and teachers the boy wanted to kill.

Maryville, Tennessee, February 24, 1999—Students told their principal that their fourteen-year-old friend had a gun. At first the student denied it, but he went on to hold the principal hostage for ninety minutes before surrendering to police. No one was injured.

Source: Associated Press, 1999.

anything to change the situation. But teens often have more power than they realize.

When violence is a serious problem, and when school officials continue to ignore it, teens need to reach outside the school community for help. Shining the light of publicity on school violence can be very effective.

Students can usually address problems in their school newspapers, but principals in most states have the power to censor stories they do not like. That is when reporters at community newspapers and television stations often get involved. Professional reporters value freedom of the press—for themselves and for responsible student reporters.

However, students should deal with the media responsibly and honestly. They should also keep in mind that rumors are not facts. Reporters appreciate factual, simple, brief stories. They also look for an angle that will interest their reading or viewing public. Home owners, for example, care about property values. Homes near violent schools are not worth as much as homes near safer schools. Similarly, senior citizens worry about their own safety.

Getting Involved in Programs That Work

Teens who get involved in school activities are usually happier at school and are better students. Being involved creates a sense of belonging and a place to go. It reduces the lure of gangs. It also presents possibilities for students who want to make their school a better place.

Most schools have some form of student government. While student representatives are often elected, it is usually possible for other students to attend meetings. Students can volunteer when there is work to be done. Participating in student government gives teens an opportunity to have a say in how their school is run.

Students can also help reduce crime at school by working with adults on advisory boards such as safe schools committees or on decision-making teams. Getting involved in groups like these helps teens develop relationships with adults that come in handy when teens need someone to listen—or to act on their behalf. Across the country, teens are getting involved in activities that directly reduce school violence. Three of these are Crime Stoppers, Teen Court, and peer mediation.

Crime Stoppers

Student Crime Stoppers programs teach students that when they report crimes or suspicious activity, "they are not snitches. They're responsible citizens," says Bob Bateman, the school safety coordinator for Guilford County, North Carolina.[6] These programs give teens a way to contact the police anonymously. Crime Stoppers operators give teens a code number. If police officers make an arrest based on information given by a teen, he or she will receive a cash reward. Many towns already have adult Crime Stoppers. Teens who are interested in creating a Crime Stoppers at their school can talk to their school resource officer or their local police department.

Teen Court

The defendant, accused of shoplifting at the mall, is a teen. So is her attorney. And the judge. Members of the jury are teens. This is teen court, an alternative justice system for first-time offenders who plead guilty to misdemeanors. If juvenile court gives permission, teens can agree to let a teen jury pass sentence. Sentences can include apologies, essays, counseling, and community service, but never jail time. Teens who are convicted almost always have to agree to sit on future juries. Most teens think it is worthwhile. Not only does Teen Court allow middle- and high-school offenders to avoid a criminal record, it also teaches them about the justice system.

A teen jury sentenced one freshman in Durham, North Carolina, to twenty-five hours of community service and attendance at three Teen Court sessions. She decided she liked it and became a regular on the jury. She also found that there were a lot of fun social activities to get involved in and a circle of new friends. The Durham Teen Court has been very successful in reducing crime, said student and Teen Court participant, Daniel Rahimtoola. "Out of the one hundred cases we've run, maybe there were five or six repeat offenders."[7]

Teen Courts across the country report an 86 percent success rate.[8] "I think teens are tough but fair with their peers," said Connie Baker, founder of the Aurora, Colorado, Teen Court. "Who knows better how to judge a kid than peers?"[9]

Peer Mediation

Emiko and Linda (not their real names) used to be pretty good friends. Then Emiko saw Linda with a guy she liked at a football game. Emiko was furious, but she did not say anything. She ignored Linda, and she would walk out of a room whenever Linda came in. Linda did not have any idea why Emiko was behaving this way. She talked to a teacher, who referred the girls for peer mediation. No one knows what went on at that meeting—peer mediators do not reveal what goes on during a session—but Emiko and Linda left the room smiling. They became best friends and stayed close all through middle school.[10]

Conflict is a fact of life. It is going to happen. So it is

important for teens to learn to deal with conflict without resorting to violence. Adults are always telling students to solve problems with words, but which words work? That is where peer mediation comes in. Peer mediation programs use peer pressure to stop school violence before it gets started. Students in conflict go to a neutral third party to help them come to their own solution to a problem.

In schools across the country, students can take their disputes to trained peer mediators who help them come up

What Happens in Peer Mediation?

- Mediators help teens establish ground rules, such as

  Make a real effort to solve the problem
  Do not use put-downs
  Do not interrupt
  Do not lie

- While each side tells what happened, mediators help students listen for facts and feelings and look at the problem in neutral terms

- Mediators help teens identify what they need in order to solve their conflict and to look for common interests

- Mediators help teens brainstorm and evaluate possible solutions and to agree on the best one

- Teens usually sign a written agreement

Source: "Teacher Talk: Peer Mediation," Indiana University Center for Adolescent Studies, June 30, 1997, <http://education.indiana.edu/cas/tt/v2i3/peer.html> (June 9, 1999).

with peaceful solutions and build or repair relationships with their classmates. Peer mediators work with problems from name-calling and hurt feelings to rumors and boyfriend or girlfriend problems. At Lincoln Junior High School in Fort Collins, Colorado, peer mediators deal with student-teacher conflicts as well. One adult and one student mediator work together to help the parties find solutions to their problems.

Peer mediators do not take on cases of bullying, sexual or racial harassment, or violence. They do not take sides. They do not give advice. And they do not mediate disputes between students they know personally. They also do not judge. They try to create a no-fault/both-fault situation in which the students can take responsibility for their behavior and the truth can emerge.

The relationship-building and communication skills that teens learn in peer mediation help create a more positive school climate one student at a time. At East Middle School in Brentwood, New York, the suspension rate went down 25 percent. Peer mediation helped reduce physical violence there, too.[11]

Students who are interested in starting a peer mediation in their school should contact the Conflict Resolution Education Network (see "How to Get Involved").

Epilogue—
No More Violence

Long after the echoes of gunfire have faded at Thurston High School in Springfield, Oregon, the pain remains.

Mikael Nickolauson and his friend Brian used to do the things all friends do. They hung out together and celebrated each other's birthdays. They traded *Star Trek* cards. They sat down with Mikael's dad and had serious discussions.

Now Mikael is gone—killed at school by a bullet from Kip Kinkel's gun. A Web site full of tributes to Mikael remains.

Mikael was his father's only son and his first-born child. He was also his father's friend. Mikael had made the transition from boy to man. He had met a girl with whom he wanted to spend the rest of his life; he had joined the Oregon National Guard to help him pay for college.

Mikael's fiancée, Michelle, says that Mikael was a very

private person who would have thought the idea of a Web site dedicated to him was funny. That was one of the reasons she loved him. She goes on with her life, aching for the guy she wanted to marry—and hoping that his death will be a reminder that everyone needs to do something to stop the violence in our society.

Never Again

The words "never again" are from a memorial statue at Dachau, a Nazi extermination camp in which thousands were killed during World War II. Mikael's friend Brian says they apply to teens today.

Teens can make the difference, he says. He begs teens to get involved with school, YMCA, clubs—anything to build a bond among people that will keep tragedies like the one that happened in Springfield from ever happening again.

Brian hopes Mikael's death will cry out to everyone—parents, teachers, police, but especially to teens. No more violence. No more deaths like Mikael's at Thurston High School.[1]

Unfortunately, Mikael's death still cries out, as do the deaths of the thirteen who died at Columbine. It is up to teens to change their schools and their lives to eliminate violence once and for all. Never again Springfield. Never again Columbine. No more violence.

How to Get Involved

Antiviolence Campaigns

Annual Day of Concern/Pledge Against Violence
Mary Lewis Grow, National Coordinator
Day of Concern about Young People and Violence
112 Nevada St.
Northfield, MN 55057
Telephone: (507) 645-5378
Fax: (507) 663-1207
E-mail: mlgrow@microassist.com
Internet: <http://www.pledge.org>

Bullying

Kids Hope
Bill Head, President
206 Bascomb Springs Court
Woodstock, GA 30189-3350
Telephone: (888) 543-7467
E-mail: gary@kidshope.org
Internet: <http://www.kidshope.org>

Kidscape
2 Grosvenor Gardens
London, England SW1W ODH
Telephone: (0171) 730-3300
Fax: (0171) 730-7081
E-mail: contact@kidscape.org.uk
Internet: <http://www.kidscape.org.uk/kidscape>

Drugs and Alcohol

Gang Resistance Education and Training (GREAT)
Thomas Scheider, Agent in Charge
Program Branch
Bureau of Alcohol, Tobacco, and Firearms
P.O. Box 50418
Washington, DC 20091-0418
Telephone: (800) 726-7070
E-mail: great@atfhq.atf.treas.gov
Internet: <http://www.atf.treas.gov/great/great/htm>

Teen Challenge International
USA Headquarters
P.O. Box 1015
Springfield, MO 65801
Telephone: (800) 814-5729
Fax: (417) 862-8209
E-mail: tcusa@teenchallengeusa.com
Internet: <http://www.teenchallenge.com>

Hate Crime

Stop the Hate
Governor's Task Force on Hate Crimes
Commonwealth of Massachusetts
Internet: <http://stopthehate.org>

Peer Mediation/Conflict Resolution

Conflict Resolution Education Network
1527 New Hampshire Ave. NW
Washington, DC 20036

Resolving Conflict Creatively Program National Center
Linda Lantieri, Director
163 Third Ave., Room 103
New York, NY 10003
Telephone: (212) 387-0225
Fax: (212) 387-0510
E-mail: esrrccp@aol.com

School Violence

Center for the Prevention of School Violence
20 Enterprise St., Suite 2
Raleigh, NC 27607-7375
Telephone: (800) 299-6054
E-mail: joanne_mcdaniel@ncsu.edu
Internet: <http://www.ncsu.edu/cpsv>

National School Safety Center
Dr. Ronald D. Stephens, Executive Director
141 Duesenberg Dr., Suite 11
Westlake Village, CA 91362
Telephone: (805) 373-9977
Fax: (805) 373-9277
E-mail: info@nssc1.org
Internet: <http://www.NSSC1.org>

Sexual Violence

Sexual Harassment: It's Not Academic
Office of Civil Rights
Department of Education
Internet: <http://www.ed.gov/offices/OCR/ocrshpam.html>

Where to Go for Help

CECP Interactive!
Advice and online discussions on school violence and mental health issues
Internet: <http://www.air.org/cecp/interact/interact.html>

Center for Substance Abuse Treatment
National Drug and Treatment Routing Service
Telephone: (800) 662-HELP

CyberAngels Confidential Tip Line
For students afraid of reprisals from school or classmates.
Cyberangels will forward tips to local authorities.
E-mail: tipline@cyberangels.org

Stop the Hate
Report a Hate Crime Online Form
Internet: <http://www.stopthehate.org>

Teen Line®
Teens Helping Teens
Telephone: (in California) (800) TLC-TEEN
(outside California) (310) 855-HOPE (collect call)
Hours: 6 P.M. to 10 P.M. daily, Pacific Standard Time

Youth Crisis Hotline: Help, Not Hassle
Telephone: (800) HIT–HOME (twenty-four hours a day)

Chapter Notes

Chapter 1. Columbine

1. Nancy Gibbs, "The Littleton Massacre," *Time*, May 3, 1999, p. 29.

2. Mark Obmascik, "Through the Eyes of Survivors," *The Denver Post*, May 13, 1999, p. A1.

3. Gibbs, p. 29.

4. John Leo, "When Life Imitates Video," *U.S. News and World Report*, May 3, 1999, p. 14.

5. Bess Keller, "Rejection and Rage Increasingly Turn Into Violence," *Associated Press/Wide World Editorial Projects in Education*, vol. 18, no. 33, 1999, p. 18.

6. Erin Emery, Steve Lipsher, and Ricky Young, "Suspects Embraced World of Darkness: Video, Poems Foreshadowed Day of Disaster," *The Denver Post*, April 22, 1999, p. A10.

7. Gibbs, p. 29.

8. Ibid., p. 36.

9. Emery, Lipsher, and Young, p. A10.

10. Lorraine Adams and Dale Russakoff, "Dissecting Columbine's Cult of the Athlete: In Search for Answers, Community Examines One Source of Killers' Rage," *Washington Post*, June 12, 1999, p. A1.

11. Interview with Jennifer (not her real name), August 1998.

12. Interview with Barbara (not her real name), July 1998.

13. Ibid.

Chapter 2. The Problem

1. Interview with Jason's father, Mr. Alexander (not his real name), May 1998.

2. Deborah Prothrow-Stith with Michaele Weissman, *Deadly Consequences: How Violence Is Destroying Our Teenage Population and a Plan to Begin Solving the Problem* (New York: HarperPerennial Library, 1993), p. 45.

3. "Content Analysis of Violence in Television," *Summary of Findings and Recommendations*, National Television Violence Study, October 23, 1997, <http://www.mediascope.org/mediascope/ntvssinfn.html> (June 9, 1999).

4. Sarah Glazner, "Violence in Schools," *CQ Researcher*, September 11, 1992, p. 802.

5. Linda Lantieri, "Waging Peace in Our Schools: Beginning with the Children," *Phi Delta Kappan*, January 1995, pp. 386–388.

6. Peter D. Hart Research Associates, *Parents, Kids, and Guns: A Nationwide Survey*, Center to Prevent Handgun Violence, 1998, <http://www.cphv.org/press/archive/oct31-98c.htm> (June 6, 1999).

7. Centers for Disease Control Surveillance Summaries, Youth Risk Behavior Surveillance–United States, 1997, Table 9, p. 8, August 14, 1998, <http://www.cdc.gov/epo/mmwr/preview/mmwrhtml/00054432.htm> (June 9, 1999).

8. Peter Hart.

9. The Student Pledge Against Gun Violence Online Pledge Count, Day of Concern about Young People and Violence, November 28, 1998, <http://www.pledge.org/total_pledges.cfm> (June 9, 1999).

10. Centers for Disease Control Surveillance Summaries, Table 24.

11. "Trends in Lifetime Prevalence of Use of Various Drugs for Eighth, Tenth and Twelfth Graders," *Monitoring the Future*, Institute for Social Research, University of Michigan, December 1997, <http://www.health.org/mtf/tables/table1a.htm> (June 9, 1999).

12. Ronald D. Stephens, "Youth Violence: Coming to a School Near You," statement at Hearing on Understanding Violent Children, U.S. House of Representatives, April 28, 1998, <http://www.nsscl.org/witness/testimon.htm> (June 9, 1999).

13. Sheila Heaviside et al., *Violence and Discipline Problems in U.S. Public Schools: 1996–97*, U.S. Department of Education, National Center for Education Statistics, NCES 98-030 (Washington, D.C.: 1998), p. 7.

14. Centers for Disease Control Surveillance Summaries, p. 9.

15. Heaviside et al., pp. 6, 8.

16. Philip Kaufman et al., *Indicators of School Crime and Safety, 1998* (Washington, D.C.: National Center for Education Statistics, Bureau of Justice Statistics, U.S. Department of Justice, 1998), p. 6.

17. Carl F. Horowitz, "Controlling School Violence," *Investor's Business Daily*, August 19, 1997, p. A1.

18. Ronald D. Stephens, testimony before the U.S. House of Representatives, April 28, 1998.

19. Kaufman, p. viii.

20. Centers for Disease Control Surveillance Summaries, p. 13.

21. Lantieri, pp. 386–388.

22. Kaufman, p. 24.

23. Terrence Stutz, "Security Expenses Surge in Urban Texas Schools," *The Dallas Morning News*, September 30, 1997, p. 1A.

Chapter 3. Trouble at School

1. Carly Milne, "Violence 101: Scared at School," *Spank! Youth Culture Online*, n.d., <http://www.spankmag.com> (May 2, 1999).

2. "Student Shot to Death in Class," *AP Online*, February 12, 1999, <http://www.elibrary.com> (June 9, 1999).

3. Marshall Croddy, "Violence Redux: A Brief Legal and Historical Perspective on Young Violence," *Social Education*, September 1997, pp. 259–260.

4. Office of Justice Programs, "Highlights of the 1996 National Youth Gang Survey Fact Sheet" (Washington, D.C.: Office of Juvenile Justice and Delinquency Programs, 1998), p. 2.

5. Cynthia Chung, Griff Palmer, and Penny Owen, "Gang Lifestyle Inspiring Crime in Smaller Towns," *Daily Oklahoman*, September 1, 1997, p. 1.

6. Office of Justice Programs.

7. Milne.

8. Chung, Palmer, and Owen, p. 1.

9. Michael O'Keefe, "Gas Forces High School to Evacuate," *Rocky Mountain News*, December 3, 1997, p. 31A.

10. Carl F. Horowitz, "Controlling School Violence," *Investor's Business Daily*, August 19, 1997, p. A1.

11. Bill Head, fax to author, January 31, 1999.

12. G. M. Batsche and H. M. Knoff, "Bullies and Their Victims: Understanding a Pervasive Problem in Our Schools," *School Psychology Review* 21, no. 2, pp. 165–174.

13. Mark Bixler, School Watch: Officials Take on Bullies," *The Atlanta Journal and Constitution*, February 4, 1999, p. J10.

14. Beverly J. Title, "Bully/Victim Violence," n.d., <http://www.krma.org/six/aav/bully.html> (June 9, 1999).

15. Dan Olweus, *Aggression in the Schools: Bullies and Whipping Boys* (New York: Hemisphere Publishing Corporation, 1978), p. 146.

16. Ibid., p. 139.

17. Title.

18. "If You Are Being Bullied," Kidscape, n.d., <http://www.kidscape.org.uk/kidscape> (June 9, 1999).

19. Head.

20. Centers for Disease Control Surveillance Summaries, "Youth Risk Behavior Surveillance—United States, 1997, *Morbidity and Mortality Weekly Report*, August 14, 1998, p. 7.

21. Thomas J. Collins, "The Fight That Never Ends Fueled by a Cycle of Revenge, Teen Violence Is at an Alarming Level in the Twin Cities," *St. Paul Pioneer Press*, December 7, 1997, p. 1A.

22. Daniel Lockwood, "Violence Among Middle School and High School Students: Analysis and Implications for Prevention," National Institute of Justice, U.S. Department of Justice, 1997, <http://www.ncjrs.org/txtfiles/166363.txt> (June 9, 1999).

23. Hate Crime Statistics, 1997, *U.S. Federal Bureau of Investigation, 1997*, <www.fbi.gov/ucr/> (June 12, 1999).

24. "Huntington Students Take Big Step With Walk for Peace: Rise in Hate Crimes Underscores Need for Such Displays," *Los Angeles Times*, April 6, 1997, Metro section, p. 6.

25. Karen Freifeld, Stacy China, and Margaret Ramirez, "Second School Attack/Cops Probe Similar Case," *Newsday*, May 22, 1997, p. A4.

26. Harris/Scholastic Research, *Hostile Hallways: The AAUW Survey on Sexual Harassment in America's Schools, 1993*, pp. 7, 14.

27. U.S. Supreme Court, *Davis v. Monroe County Board of Education*, n.d. (abstract), <http://oyez.nwu.edu/cases/cases.cgi?command=show&case_id=474&page=abstract > (October 24, 1999).

28. Rhode Island Task Force on Gay, Lesbian, Bisexual, and Transgendered Youth, *Rhode Island Safe Schools Report*, "School Shouldn't Hurt: Lifting the Burden From Gay, Lesbian, Bisexual, and Transgendered Youth," March 1996, <http://members.tripod.com/~twood/safeschools.html> (June 9, 1999).

29. Lauren Dodge, "Suspect Once Voted Most Likely to Start World War III," *AP Online*, May 22, 1998, <http://www.elibrary.com> (October 24, 1999).

30. Jeff Barnard, "Second Student Dies From Wounds in Ore. Shooting," *AP Online*, May 22, 1998, <http://www.elibrary.com> (October 24, 1999).

31. David Foster, "The Warning Signs Were Many Before the School Rampage," *AP Online*, May 22, 1998, <http://www.elibrary.com> (October 24, 1999).

32. National Education Association, "Inside Scoop: What Can We Do About Violence?", *NEA Today Online*, September 1998, <http://www.nea.org/9809/scoop.html> (June 9, 1999).

Chapter 4. Making School a Better Place

1. *Break the Silence, Stop the Violence* page, Hopkinsville High School, 1997, <www.geocities.com/toto?s=19190039> (June 9, 1999).

2. Interview with Jennifer (not her real name), May 1995.

3. Mark Fritz, "Alienated Teens Empathize With High School Gunmen/Violence: Although Appalled by Colorado Slayings, Many Blame Cliquish Subculture Within Institutions," *Los Angeles Times*, April 28, 1999, p. A1.

4. Interview with Steve (not his real name), August 20, 1998.

5. National Education Association, "Inside Scoop: What Can We Do About Violence?" *NEA Today Online*, September 1998, <http://www.nea.org/neatoday/9809/scoop.html> (June 9, 1999).

6. "School Violence Down in State: A School Official Says Supervision and Parental Cooperation Are Among Reasons for the Decrease," *Fayetteville Observer Times*, January 13, 1998, p. A1.

7. David Blocher, "Jury of Peers Determines Teens' Fate at Teen Court," *Falcon's Cry Online*, Jordan High School, Durham, North Carolina, May 1998, <www.jordan.durham.k-12.nc.us/fc/may1998/teencourt.html> (June 9, 1999).

8. Paul Hinman, "A Jury of Their Peers: Teen Court Offers Youth a Chance to Be Understood," *Wisconsin State Journal*, August 2, 1997, p. 3B.

9. Cindy Brovsky, "Teen Court Pioneer Offers Award-Winning Argument," *The Denver Post*, November 13, 1998, p. A25.

10. Interview with Rick Arthur, March 1999.

11. Bill Kaufman, "Students Work Out Differences Through Talk," *Newsday*, October 16, 1996, p. E18.

Epilogue—No More Violence

1. Michael A. Nickolauson, Brian Jones, and Michelle Calhoun, "Thurston High School Shooting: A Comprehensive Web Page About the Thurston Event," *Mikael Nickolauson Tribute Page*, n.d., <http://www.thurston.5g.com/nickolauson.htm> (June 5, 1999).

Further Reading

Akins, S. Beth. *Voices from the Street: Young Former Gang Members Tell Their Stories*. Boston: Little, Brown & Company, 1996.

Banfield, Susan. *Ethnic Conflicts in Schools*. Hillside, N.J.: Enslow Publishers, 1995.

Carter, Jimmy. *Talking Peace: A Vision for the Next Generation*. New York: Dutton Children's Books, 1995.

Crews, Gordon A., and M. Reid Counts. *The Evolution of School Disturbance in America: Colonial Times to Modern Day*. Westport, Conn.: Greenwood Publishing Group, 1997.

Lantieri, Linda, and Janet Patti. *Waging Peace in Our Schools*. New York: Ballantine Books, 1996.

LeShan, Eda. *When Kids Drive Kids Crazy: How to Get Along with Your Friends & Enemies*. New York: Dial, 1990.

Prothrow-Stith, Deborah, with Michaele Weissman. *Deadly Consequences: How Violence Is Destroying Our Teenage Population and a Plan to Begin Solving the Problem*. New York: HarperPerennial Library, 1993.

Radcliffe, Rebecca R. *About to Burst: Handling Stress & Ending Violence—A Message for Youth*. Minneapolis: EASE, 1999.

Internet Sites

Anti-Defamation League: Stop Hate
<http://www.adl.org/hate-patrol/1.html>

Center for the Prevention of School Violence
<http://www.ncsu.edu/cpsv>

Early Warning, Timely Responses: A Guide to Safe Schools
<http://www.air.org/cecp/guide/Default.htm>

Learning Exchange: Understanding and Combating School Violence
<http://homer.lalc.k12.ca.us/essay/4_3/svresource.html>

National Center for Education Statistics
<http://nces.ed.gov/>

National Youth Gang Center
<http://www.iir.com/nygc>

Office of Juvenile Justice and Delinquency Prevention: School Violence Resources
<http://ojjdp.ncjrs.org/resources/school.html>

U.S. Department of Education: Safe and Drug Free Schools Program
<http://www.ed.gov/offices/OESE/SDFS>

Index